821
MACE

THE FLOWE

GM0037480\

MEDBH McGUCKIAN

The Flower Master

Oxford New York

OXFORD UNIVERSITY PRESS

1982

Oxford University Press, Walton Street, Oxford OX2 6DP

London Glasgow New York Toronto
Delhi Bombay Calcutta Madras Karachi
Kuala Lumpur Singapore Hong Kong Tokyo
Nairobi Dar es Salaam Cape Town
Melbourne Auckland

and associates in
Beirut Berlin Ibadan Mexico City Nicosia

© Medbh McGuckian 1980, 1981, 1982

All rights reserved. No part of this publication may be reproduced,
stored in a retrieval system, or transmitted, in any form or by any means,
electronic, mechanical, photocopying, recording, or otherwise, without
the prior permission of Oxford University Press

This book is sold subject to the condition that it shall not, by way
of trade or otherwise, be lent, re-sold, hired out or otherwise circulated
without the publisher's prior consent in any form of binding or cover
other than that in which it is published and without a similar condition
including this condition being imposed on the subsequent purchaser

British Library Cataloguing in Publication Data

McGuckian Medbh
The flower master.
I. Title.
821'.914   PR6063.A234/
ISBN 0-19-211949-4

Library of Congress Cataloging in Publication Data

McGuckian, Medbh, 1950–
The flower master.
I. Title.
PR6063.C5F59 1982 821'.914   81–19005
ISBN 0-19-211949-4 (pbk.) AACR2

Set by King's English Typesetters Ltd
Printed in Great Britain

For John and Liam

Acknowledgements

Acknowledgements are due to the editors of the following, in which some of these poems first appeared: *The Ulster Tatler, Bananas, Stone Ferry Review, Fortnight, Outposts, London Magazine, Quarto, The Listener, The Times Literary Supplement, The Poetry Book Society Christmas Supplement* (1981), *Gown Magazine*, Queen's University, Belfast. Poems were also included in the pamphlet 'Single Ladies' (Interim Press), the pamphlet 'Portrait of Joanna' (Ulsterman Publications); in *Trio Poetry 2* (1981) (Blackstaff Press), in *New Poetry 5* (Arts Council of Great Britain), and in *Poetry Introduction 5* (1982) (Faber and Faber). In 1979 'The Flitting' won First Prize in the National Poetry Competition.

Contents

That Year

That year it was something to do with your hands:
To play about with rings, to harness rhythm
In staging bleach or henna on the hair,
Or shackling, unshackling the breasts.

I remembered as a child the red kite
Lost forever over our heads, the white ball
A pin-prick on the tide, and studied
The leaf-patterned linoleum, the elaborate

Stitches on my pleated bodice.
It was like a bee's sting or a bullet
Left in me, this mark, this sticking pins in dolls,
Listening for the red and white

Particles of time to trickle slow, like a wet nurse
Feeding nonchalantly someone else's child.
I wanted curtainings, and cushionings;
The grass is no bed after dark.

BELFAST PUBLIC LIBRARIES SCHOOLS

Tulips

Touching the tulips was a shyness
I had had for a long time – such
Defensive mechanisms to frustrate the rain
That shakes into the sherry-glass
Of the daffodil, though scarcely
Love's young dream; such present-mindedness
To double-lock in tiers as whistle-tight,
Or catch up on sleep with cantilevered
Palms cupping elbows. It's their independence
Tempts them to this grocery of soul.

Except, like all governesses, easily
Carried away, in sunny
Absences of mirrors they exalt themselves
To ballets of revenge, a kind
Of twinness, an olympic way of earning,
And are sacrificed to plot, their faces
Lifted many times to the artistry of light –
Its lovelessness a deeper sort
Of illness than the womanliness
Of tulips with their bee-dark hearts.

Problem Girl

I'm a sitter-out in a darkened room,
Eating an apple and thinking about
Celery, oysters and chocolate.

The problem girl will daydream
To the music of the jossed boutique
On Saturday afternoons.

In my first sleep, I see in the glass
The man who washed in a southward stream
Where three lands meet, climbing my plaited ladder,

And, just as socially, dropping out of the picture
Into a dream of cowboy boots –
I should tell the bees, my five pointed stars.

The Chain Sleeper

Unshameable this leggy girl who sleeps and sleeps
In china duck-down, one breast bigger than the other.
She dresses under her dressing-gown, her fussy perfume
Eating into all the storyable floors of blue.

To the naked eye of the brainy shower she is
All one midnight goddess; the roomy shoals of her hair
A million scarves in the billowy schools of thought.
She lives in lifts of the first water, wanting to be usual.

Such semi-precious stones the longshore whittles.
They lie on split-level waste tips, banding in volcanoes
Like potatoes; their careers are cut and dried,
For costume jewellery, for other people's keeping.

Admiring the Furs

Admiring the furs in the window
Is just about as close as we get.
It is what they are like in summer I want to know.

At the checkpoints it occurs to me,
My measurements at nine,
My secret box stuffed with peacock's feathers.

I sit light at the roundabouts,
Crying into myself,
I've been here for all the houses being built –

Not ordinarily scattered,
As a man keeps all his women,
Holding tidily to all their echoed hands –

Preoccupied, not realizing
Sneaking away in a slow
Agonizing death is as painful a death as it is.

Mr McGregor's Garden

Some women save their sanity with needles.
I complicate my life with studies
Of my favourite rabbit's head, his vulgar volatility,
Or a little ladylike sketching
Of my resident toad in his flannel box;
Or search for handsome fungi for my tropical
Herbarium, growing dry-rot in the garden,
And wishing that the climate were kinder,
Turning over the spiky purple heads among the moss
With my cheese-knife to view the slimy veil.

Unlike the cupboard-love of sleepers in the siding,
My hedgehog's sleep is under his control
And not the weather's; he can rouse himself
At half-an-hour's notice in the frost, or leave at will
On a wet day in August, by the hearth.
He goes by breathing slowly, after a large meal,
A lively evening, very cross if interrupted,
And returns with a hundred respirations
To the minute, weak and nervous when he wakens,
Busy with his laundry.

On sleepless nights while learning
Shakespeare off by heart,
I feel that Bunny's at my bedside
In a white cotton nightcap,
Tickling me with his whiskers.

The Long Engagement

i

In my all-weather loneliness I am like a sparrow
Picking leftovers of rice in a mortar,
A dark cicada clinging to a branch,
The empty space created by your kiss;

Occasionally, as Sunday silver, sit
In a quiet, eastward-facing room,
And make a thread from the fibres of the five signs
Leading to the eight valleys, my lush palace gate.

ii

I lie down thirsty from the thunderstorm,
Visualizing first this book, the objects on the tray,
Then you asleep, my loosening
Towards your pointed ceiling,

Through half-open lids your hand,
Repeat your name, and count the laddered
Steps to your house, till I fall
Backwards through the salted folds, the spring of your door.

iii

You overflow, sleeping on your back:
My lap is bent upon itself, my bulbs
Are fleeced, my wishbone wings are tied.

Perhaps my worry beads need sanding –
All they ask is to be lifted from their winding
Cold, the subsidence of their avenues.

Lychees

You wonder at that Georgian terrace
Miles out of town where the motorway begins.
My great-grandfather was a coachman,
And knew how far away he was in the dark
By mysteries of the Rosary. My grandmother said
You could tell a good husband
By the thumbed leaves of his prayer-book.

A dead loss, my mother counts you,
Setting my teeth on edge at all hours,
Getting me to break the lychee's skin.
She underestimates the taste of sacrifice,
The irrelevance of distances,
Cat's-eyes, the cleanness of hands.

The Hollywood Bed

We narrow into the house, the room, the bed,
Where sleep begins its shunting. You adopt
Your mask, your intellectual cradling of the head,
Neat as notepaper in your creaseless
Envelope of clothes, while I lie crosswise,
Imperial as a favoured only child,
Calmed by sagas of how we lay like spoons
In a drawer, till you blew open
My tightened bud, my fully-buttoned housecoat,
Like some Columbus mastering
The saw-toothed waves, the rows of letter 'm's'.

Now the headboard is disturbed
By your uncomfortable skew, your hands
Like stubborn adverbs visiting your face,
Or your shoulder, in your piquancy of dreams,
The outline that if you were gone,
Would find me in your place.

The Retired Couple

I have graduated to the perennial odour
Of the separate bed, this linen prison
Where I hear your heavy brushing
Like an icy river in the next room,
Making despicable noises nobody favours.

And your voice blurred as a prayer
Through my famished hesitation,
My irrelevant solidity, the damp
That gathers over the summer
In the backyard crevices like milk-tooth decay.

But who could disinfect or dust it now
That I am used to my own company,
The special touch of my tools you interfere with,
Deciduous as the village-people papering our walls,
The sea-blue water that the supplement showed us?

The Sofa

Do not be angry if I tell you
Your letter stayed unopened on my table
For several days. If you were friend enough
To believe me, I was about to start writing
At any moment; my mind was savagely made up,
Like a serious sofa moved
Under a north window. My heart, alas,

Is not the calmest of places.
Still it is not my heart that needs replacing:
And my books seem real enough to me,
My disasters, my surrenders, all my loss . . .
Since I was child enough to forget
That you loathe poetry, you ask for some –
About nature, greenery, insects, and of course,

The sun – surely that would be to open
An already open window? Celebrating
The impudence of flowers? If I could
Interest you instead in his large, gentle stares,
How his soft shirt is the inside of pleasure
To me, why I must wear white for him,
Imagine he no longer trembles

When I approach, no longer buys me
Flowers for my name day . . . But I spread
On like a house, I begin to scatter
To a tiny to-and-fro at odds
With the wear on my threshold. Somewhere
A curtain rising wonders where I am,
My books sleep, pretending to forget me.

Ducks and Drakes

By the stone in his hand I tested my desire
Which I wouldn't trust as far as he could throw it,
Locked in sky, picking and choosing its visits to the water,
Till it sank without the hope of ever surfacing
Into the rockery he determined to have spoken for
At such a crucial distance from himself.

Not that freedom was its chauffeur from the arbitrary shore,
Like something falling off a cake, the arc
His body had to make, or that I needed persuading
Even my frowns were beautiful, my tenable
Emotions largely playing with themselves,
To be laid like a table set for breakfast.

Slips

The studied poverty of a moon roof,
The earthenware of dairies cooled by apple trees,
The apple tree that makes the whitest wash . . .

But I forget names, remembering them wrongly
Where they touch upon another name,
A town in France like a woman's Christian name.

My childhood is preserved as a nation's history,
My favourite fairy tales the shells
Leased by the hermit crab.

I see my grandmother's death as a piece of ice,
My mother's slimness restored to her,
My own key slotted in your door –

Tricks you might guess from this unfastened button,
A pen mislaid, a word misread,
My hair coming down in the middle of a conversation.

To My Grandmother

I would revive you with a swallow's nest:
For as long a time as I could hold my breath
I would feel your pulse like tangled weeds
Separate into pearls. The heart should rule
The summer, ringing like a sickle over
The need to make life hard. I would
Sedate your eyes with rippleseed, those
Hollow points that close as if
Your eyelids had been severed to
Deny you sleep, imagine you a dawn.
I would push a chrysanthemum stone
Into your sleeve without your noticing
Its reaching far, its going, its returning.
When the end of summer comes, it is
A season by itself; when your tongue
Curls back like a sparrow's buried head,
I would fill your mouth with rice and mussels.

The Seed-Picture

This is my portrait of Joanna – since the split
The children come to me like a dumb-waiter,
And I wonder where to put them, beautiful seeds
With no immediate application . . . the clairvoyance
Of seed-work has opened up
New spectrums of activity, beyond a second home.
The seeds dictate their own vocabulary,
Their dusty colours capture
More than we can plan,
The mould on walls, or jumbled garages,
Dead flower heads where insects shack . . .
I only guide them not by guesswork
In their necessary numbers,
And attach them by the spine to a perfect bedding,
Woody orange pips, and tear-drop apple,
The banana of the caraway, wrinkled pepper-corns,
The pocked peach, or waterlily honesty,
The seamed cherry stone so hard to break.

Was it such self-indulgence to enclose her
In the border of a grandmother's sampler,
Bonding all the seeds in one continuous skin,
The sky resolved to a cloud the length of a man?
To use tan linseed for the trees, spiky
Sunflower for leaves, bright lentils
For the window, patna stars
For the floral blouse? Her hair
Is made of hook-shaped marigold, gold
Of pleasure for her lips, like raspberry grain.
The eyelids oatmeal, the irises
Of Dutch blue maw, black rape
For the pupils, millet
For the vicious beige circles underneath.
The single pearl barley
That sleeps around her dullness
Till it catches light, makes women
Feel their age, and sigh for liberation.

The Sun-Trap

Our lean-to greenhouse lends
Quite a sun-trap in the mornings,
Where I page you from this sickly Irish weather.
And the hygroscope says 'orchid',
Though in winter it stays blue,
Unless placed between the window and the storm-sash.

I am touched by even the strange gesture
Of rain stopping, your penetration
Of my mask of 'bon viveur', my crested notepaper,
My lined envelopes. From your last letter
I construed at least the word
For kisses, if not quite a kindred spirit.

But my night has been chequered
By toothache, and your reference
To the magically fertile German girl
Who sleeps in the bunk above you
At the workcamp. She seems
To me quite flirtatious

Though you say she's the sort of girl
You'd rather have as a daughter –
Which reminds me of my cousin once-removed,
And the near-tragedy
Of our long pony-trekking weekend . . .
You find it odd I should resurrect him

Just when I seemed
To be losing the urge to discuss him?
My wholesome curiosity in corpses?
Miles from anywhere, if you could learn
From other people's letters to me,
We might talk like human beings are supposed to.

Gentians

In my alpine house, the slavery I pay
My wilful gentians! exploring all their pleats
And tucks as though they had something precious
Deep inside, that beard of camel-hair
In the throat. I watch them
Ease their heads so slowly
Through their thumbhole necklines, till they sit
Like tailors in their earth shoes,
Their watery husbands' knots. No insects
Visit them, nor do their ovaries swell,
Yet every night in Tibet their seeds
Are membraned by the snow, their roots
Are bathed by the passage of melt-water;
They tease like sullen spinsters
The dewfall of summer limes.

The Orchid House

A flower's fragrance is a woman's virtue;
So I tell them underground in pairs,
Or in their fleshy white sleeves, how
Desirable their shapes, how one
Was lost for sixty years, with all
Its arching spikes, its honeyed tessellations,
And how in bloom they will resemble
Moths, the gloss of mirrors, Christmas
Stars, their helmets blushing
Red-brown when they marry.

Your House

Our childless house has perfect teeth.
The running water of its lovemaking
Is pickled in silence, in a wicker-covered
Bottle, its fluorescence steadying itself
Into the barely breatheable importance
Even your servants' quarters nudge away,
Where you afford your matted walk-through
Rooms, with their creamy hems, their windows
Succouring the heart. The way they swing
Like the sickled gladiolus, swell your house
As Ireland's tiny mountains load her breast
Like a necklace! How they take the rain
In their eyes, and make all possible use
Of moonlight, as a sea-meadow
Becomes a bath of meadow-sweet
Under the goats' milk stars, till you might
Ring your bells, knowing someone would come.

Distance

It is not in our interest to be too attractive:
The frequent death of distant suns
That prey upon these sexless nights
Leaves me incapable of dream as birds.

An unobtrusive glance will trace
The far-off mocking star, the character
Shone by a flower on your neck, the shallow
Seconds between obligation and dawn.

The Soil-Map

I am not a woman's man, but I can tell,
By the swinging of your two-leaf door,
You are never without one man in the shadow
Of another; and because the mind
Of a woman between two men is lighter
Than a spark, the petalled steps to your porch
Feel frigid with a lost warmth. I will not
Take you in hardness, for all the dark cage
Of my dreaming over your splendid fenestration,
Your moulded sills, your slender purlins,

The secret woe of your gutters. I will do it
Without niggardliness, like food with one
Generous; a moment as auspicious
And dangerous as the christening of a ship,
My going in to find the settlement
Of every floor, the hump of water
Following the moon, and her discolouring,
The saddling derangement of a roof
That might collapse its steepness
Under the sudden strain of clearing its name.

For anyone with patience can divine
How your plasterwork has lost key, the rendering
About to come away. So like a rainbird,
Challenged by a charm of goldfinch,
I appeal to the god who fashions edges
Whether such turning-points exist
As these saltings we believe we move
Away from, as if by simply shaking
A cloak we could disbud ourselves,
Dry out, and cease to live there?

I have found the places on the soil-map,
Proving it possible once more to call
Houses by their names, Annsgift or Mavisbank,
Mount Juliet or Bettysgrove: they should not
Lie with the gloom of disputes to interrupt them
Every other year, like some disease
Of language making humorous the friendship
Of the thighs. I drink to you as Hymenstown,
(My touch of fantasy) or First Fruits,
Impatient for my power as a bride.

The Swing

It's been quite a year for strange weather.
From speedy March to slow September,
The drought left firemen sleepless, Ireland
So like Italy Italians came to film it.
Each evening the Egyptian goddess
Swallowed the sun, her innocent
Collective pleasure, never minding his violent temper,
His copious emissions, how he sprinkled
The lawn of space till it became
A deadly freckled junkyard.

Looking at what is most important
Leaves me blind: without leaving my room
I might escape from waves in a Roman cage–cup
Made from a single piece of glass, and sail
My wafer yacht on the solar wind, my watered
Body, my earthy liquid centre, protected
By a crown. Wish me a mission
Trouble free; if I lose contact,
To die smiling of exhaustion, the invisible
Child upon a swing so I can almost touch his hands.

The Sunbench

Behind my party wall what bolts of silk
Prepare their images, relax from them
Like petals lolling in a knot garden
Voluptuous with rapid growth! These seed leaves
I have summered and these true leaves wintered
Through the spartan frost, supported by sweet
Chestnut, riven oak, till lime unlocks
Their mongrel tenderness, the shattering excretion of the
      rose . . .

This is not the hardness of a single night,
A rib that I could clearly do without. It is
The room where you have eaten daily,
Shaking free like a hosting tree, the garden
Shaking off the night's weak appetite,
The sunbench brown and draining into fallow.

The Katydid

The Little Orchid saw from Pewter Lane
The Forbidden City beyond the Jade Canal,
Its roofs of yellow tile, the hawks around
The Gate of Western Flowering.

On soft clogs she crawled to the Emperor's side,
A total eclipse with her apple-head,
Her water-chestnut eyes, the charm of the katydid,
The white tiger, the fragrant bamboo.

Now she sails her marble picnic boat
In the garden of Aquatic Grasses,
Listening to the opening of the lotus buds,
Her honeysuckle lotions in wicker trays:

The raw silk caravan route
Escorts her changeable dresses,
Her yellow china packed like shoes,
The paper servant world.

The Empress Dowager tried and failed to abolish foot-binding
in nineteenth-century China.

Champagne

The soulless matchmaking of lunar moths,
Uncanny, delicate or helpful, dove-coloured
Bosoms in the night: their fictions hurt us
Gently, like the nudity of rose-beige tea-gowns . . .

The mayflies' opera is their only moon, only
Those that fall on water reproduce, content
With scattering in fog or storm, such ivory
As elephants hold lofty, like champagne.

The Flower Master

Like foxgloves in the school of the grass moon
We come to terms with shade, with the principle
Of enfolding space. Our scissors in brocade,
We learn the coolness of straight edges, how
To gently stroke the necks of daffodils
And make them throw their heads back to the sun.

We slip the thready stems of violets, delay
The loveliness of the hibiscus dawn with quiet ovals,
Spirals of feverfew like water splashing,
The papery legacies of bluebells. We do
Sea-fans with sea-lavender, moon-arrangements
Roughly for the festival of moon-viewing.

This black container calls for sloes, sweet
Sultan, dainty nipplewort, in honour
Of a special guest, who summoned to the
Tea ceremony, must stoop to our low doorway,
Our fontanelle, the trout's dimpled feet.

The Butterfly Farm

The film of a butterfly ensures that it is dead:
Its silence like the green cocoon of the car-wash,
Its passion for water to uncloud.

In the Japanese tea house they believe
In making the most of the bright nights:
That the front of a leaf is male, the back female.

There are grass stains on their white stockings;
In artificial sun even the sound are disposable;
The mosaic of their wings is spun from blood.

Cyanide in the killing-jar relaxes the Indian moon moth,
The pearl-bordered beauty, the clouded yellow,
The painted lady, the silver-washed blue.

Fossils

This is in fact our only record of them,
As if they had found a breathing, a flotation chamber
Here in the mud, uncrushed as other
Fashionable experiments, these maturing
Soft-bodied males, no oxygen
Fuelling the cells of their decay.

Encountering no change, they see
No cause for change, as mantled
As the eggs in the paper cradle shell
The octopus secretes from his arm –
Bizarre their chemistry, their florid junctions,
Under our straightened gaze their rounding eyes.

The Dowry Murder

The danger of biscuit-coloured silk
Is how it just reveals you, the chill
Of the balloon material swaying
In the wind that is not there – the part
Of my body that deals with it needs churching,
Where I keep secret house, a room within
A room, or an organic, touch-dry garden
Where I sit upon my hair. From deep-set
Windows I contemplate the immature moon
Upon the louvered roof of the orangery,
The snow-well thatched with straw, my
Moorish fabrics sapient with
My love of heavy clothing.
Though my railway novel ends
With the bride's sari catching fire
While cooking succotash, something about
The light that is just there musters
A last kiss, your clutch on my ordinary stem,
Then your head falling off into a drawer.

The Witchmark

You paint, Miss Churchill? Pray go on.
Then you would know a dangerous face.
How spirit lusts towards us as we to it, like
The play of different lights. Your body,
That naked altar, how would you show
Behind a picnic, gloves and violets, its readiness
To be roused, its hopeless snow? Or in the cloudiness
Above a house, how heaven was beginning
To look less like the sky and more like the soul
Of the woman that wished to live there,
Wished it to outlast her? My intended is poor,
And, at the minute, head over ears in Cromwell;
He is like an interim desk I have never got round
To replacing, or imagined to be there in order
To be rejected. He would not encourage
The future to hurry, yet he told me
He had once conjured a book out of a chest,
Written in red, and once between compline
And twilight he had heard two light
Dancing steps by a girl. I find this
Oppressive, the suggestion of a neighbourhood
Beyond the grave, yet I confess a room,
A street, a meadow may become unsure,
A door untouched may close, a lover's hand
Became malicious, pointing out the witchmark
On his tongue. My mother's deathbed
Was prolonged and poetic, oh, those fatal
Coughs, how could they be so great without
Being greater? I thought the idea of torture
Was to help the truth, and so, dry-eyed,
She also waited, for some utter alteration,
Or for singing bread. And finally, a voice,
She said, had woken her, giving me her
Only loveless look, my last resort
Her amatory flower-heads that never died.

The Standing

This is my day-by-day book, my open-air
Oratory, of that tenacious month, so little
News, uncertain weather, I began to see
Light through the curtains of my sick-room.

My godmother, an understanding kinswoman,
Had taught me, her namesake, almost natural
Daughter, cushion-making—Irish stitch
On cloth-of-silver – how to restring

Loose drop-shaded pearls, such static
Occupations . . . I remembered keeping silkworms
As a little girl, my everlasting embroidery;
How my mother lay with me, her surreptitious

Kindness . . . I remember her face of that day,
Its sleep enforced like malefactors
Lodged in the lowest storey of the keep,

The Pagan Tower: her feet just clear
Of a recumbent lamb, her dress unwrinkled
Like the Rhône passing through Geneva.

The Moon Pond

I thought this morning of my yellowed Juliette cap,
Its head-dress of artificial pearls that I wore once,
And never wore again . . . It is not the same
With this bright moon pond where, they say,
If you come once you'll likely come again,
Fed slowly by the natural canal, where swims the otter
You were dreaming had made you pregnant.

As with an egg I close my mouth, with an egg
I open it again, my May Day rising, after
My warrior's sleep, and crossing the fat churchyard
Left by a green Christmas, the souls of the dead
As thick as bees in an uncut meadow round me.
I leave a bowl of spring water womanly on the table
For your wild and nameless sprays before they withered.

I leave a stack of salt fallen from a thimble,
A measure of milk with a cock's step of butter,
Coming in hills and going in mountains:
For this milk-fevered lady is the round-eyed child
Listening with bated breath to the singalong
Of birds that, waking in the heart of rain,
Would just as boldly start to mate again.

Next Day Hill

Who knows, you might receive in time for Christmas
A book with primrose edges and a mirror
In the cover. Like a room decorated
At different periods, you will feel it
Like a draught, a shaft of white coming
Long-postponed out of a blue room,
The thin, straight stalk of a woman. It is when
One tries to recount a dream, going on,
Going on, the shyness of other people
Stops mattering, you put it in a cage

Until your lips are quite rested. Is this
Treating a friendship like glass, this great
Temptation to unfold the labour
One had to go through to get back
To the proper size? I wanted so much
To get down again to a place full of old
Summers, Mexican hats, soft fruitwood
Furniture, and less moon, the porch-light
And the leaves catching one another's glance,
Firm clouds not pulled out of shape by wind.

But I am writing here in the dark
Purple sitting room, the buttons scarcely meeting
On my pink shirt with the pearl collar,
The baby near the stove feeding
Strawberries to our ancient tortoise,
As if neither could go to the other:
Upstairs, the hard beds, the dimity
Curtains, the dreadful viking strain
Of the study's brick floor where
My poems thicken in the desk.

I am waiting like a sundowner
For the gift of all travel, the first
Steering star, or a man turned down
Forever by the only girl – call her
Elizabeth, he soaks himself in the comfort
Of her name till a kind of mist
Covers the sky that's all exposed,
A gallant white, inside and out,
And gathers its spine to wedge itself
Somewhere tight, beyond the reach of the mirror.

The Perfect Mother

Nature is a child that calls
Through the segments of his sleep for you
To put away his things in the night.

I know this fatherly stretching
Of the arms, or washing of the feet,
The hands, is reconciliation – hands

That might, if we could touch them,
Tell us much about each other, maybe
Even whether the day is wet or dry.

But here we watch like hawks
Until the morning goes with kindness,
Like the intercourse of rivers, irreversible

As dawn, and fall to stimulate
Whatever seems the lightest kind of sleep,
The sulky wanderings of Jews.

The Aphrodisiac

She gave it out as if it were
A marriage or a birth, some other
Interesting family event, that she
Had finished sleeping with him, that
Her lover was her friend. It was his heart
She wanted, the bright key to his study,
Not the menacings of love. So he is
Banished to his estates, to live
Like a man in a glasshouse; she has taken to
A little cap of fine white lace
In the mornings, feeds her baby
In a garden you could visit blindfold
For its scent alone:
                    But though a ray of grace
Has fallen, all her books seem as frumpish
As the last year's gambling game, when she
Would dress in pink taffeta, and drive
A blue phaeton, or in blue, and drive
A pink one, with her black hair supported
By a diamond comb, floating about
Without panniers. How his most
Caressing look, his husky whisper suffocates her,
This almost perfect power of knowing
More than a kept woman. The between-maid
Tells me this is not the only secret staircase.
Rumour has it she's taken to rouge again.

The Theatre

This is our second friendship, recent
And jealous, a treaty cold
As your distrust of music.
Though you understand
Poetry better than men, I trust your tongue
As I would a stone that thirsts after the weather,
Little stay-at-home, living without
Perfecting itself.

You are always hungry, not made
For prison; you have no handwriting
Because you never write. Yours is the readership
Of the rough places where I make
My sweet refusals of you, your
Natural violence.

So with the best sort of thankfulness,
I throw the window romantically open
To let sleep out of the room, or the possibility
My poems might have perished. Would
They last even as long
As the sun's burn on your arm?

I do not reproach the sky
For its answer. If you had a boat,
You would name it Socrates, perhaps,
After yourself, and tell me
How I live in poems, or how
Far away I was
In the bad light, on the stage of the summer theatre.

Power-Cut

The moon is salmon as a postage-stamp
Over the tonsured trees, a rise-and-fall lamp
In a cracked ice ceiling. The cruelty
Of road conditions flushes summer near,
As the storm seal hangs along the pier.

My dishes on the draining-board
Lie at an even keel, the baby lowered
Into his lobster-pot pen; my sponge
Disintegrates in water like a bird's nest,
A permanent wave gone west.

These plotted holes of days my keep-net shades,
Soluble as refuse in canals; the old flame
Of the candle sweats in the night, its hump
A dowager's with bones running thin:
The door-butler lets the strangers in.

The Flitting

'You wouldn't believe all this house has cost me –
In body-language terms, it has turned me upside down.'
I've been carried from one structure to the other
On a chair of human arms, and liked the feel
Of being weightless, that fraternity of clothes . . .
Now my own life hits me in the throat, the bumps
And cuts of the walls as telling
As the poreholes in strawberries, tomato seeds.
I cover them for safety with these Dutch girls
Making lace, or leaning their almond faces
On their fingers with a mandolin, a dreamy
Chapelled ease abreast this other turquoise-turbanned,
Glancing over her shoulder with parted mouth.

She seems a garden escape in her unconscious
Solidarity with darkness, clove-scented
As an orchid taking fifteen years to bloom,
And turning clockwise as the honeysuckle.
Who knows what importance
She attaches to the hours?
Her narrative secretes its own values, as mine might
If I painted the half of me that welcomes death
In a faggotted dress, in a peacock chair,
No falser biography than our casual talk
Of losing a virginity, or taking a life, and
No less poignant if dying
Should consist in more than waiting.

I postpone my immortality for my children,
Little rock-roses, cushioned
In long-flowering sea-thrift and metrics,
Lacking elemental memories:
I am well-earthed here as the digital clock,
Its numbers flicking into place like overgrown farthings
On a bank where once a train
Ploughed like an emperor living out a myth
Through the cambered flesh of clover and wild carrot.

The Gardener

Most like there was an orchard where my woodlot stands,
Kept by some turn-of-the-century gardener who knew
The ways of birds, how sparrows cannot open sunflower pods,
How ash-trees will bring finches to your gate; who trained
The fruiting arms of ever-bearing raspberries, and covered them
With cottonseed and cheesecloth through the see-sawing
Temperatures of March, till honey-dipped, they strained
As low as Driscoll's muscadines, the wineberries you gather
On Meeting House Road without getting out of your car.

No wren has darkened the door of my wren-hut, though I make
Pin-money from my young tomato plants, return a little sea-
    struck
From my fall trips through the Pine Barrens, or the Finger
    Lakes:
I could stage a breakdown, smash my blue jardinière,
My hen-on-nest, my amber-bottled vitamins, or else
Revolve the classics in the bookcase from my nursing chair
Till I'd be born again into that warless world, and think
I loved him, entering the parlour at noon, unattended,
With 'The Voice that Breathed o'er Eden' being sung.

The Heiress

You say I should stay out of the low
Fields; though my hands love dark,
I should creep till they are heart-shaped,
Like Italian rooms no longer hurt by sun.

When I look at the striped marble of the glen,
I see the husbandry of a good spadesman,
Lifting without injury, or making sure
Where the furrow is this year, the ridge
Will be the next; and my pinched grain,
Hanging like a window on the smooth spot
Of a mountain, or a place for fawns, watches
Your way with horses, your delicate adam work.

But I am lighter of a son, through my slashed
Sleeves the inner sleeves of purple keep remembering
The moment exactly, remembering the birth
Of an heiress means the gobbling of land.

I tell you, dead leaves do not necessarily
Fall; it is not coldness, but the tree itself
That bids them go, preventing their destruction.
So I walk along the beach, unruly, I drop
Among my shrubbery of seaweed my black acorn buttons.

BELFAST PUBLIC LIBRARIES SCHOOLS

The Mast Year

Some kinds of trees seem ever eager
To populate new ground, the oak or pine.
Though beech can thrive on many soils
And carve itself an empire, its vocation
Is gentler; it casts a shade for wildflowers
Adapted to the gloom, which feed
Like fungus on its rot of bedstraw leaves.

It makes an awkward neighbour, as the birch
Does, that lashes out in gales, and fosters
Intimacy with toadstools, till they sleep
In the benevolence of each other's smells,
Never occupying many sites for long:
The thin red roots of alder vein
The crumbled bank, the otter's ruptured door.

Bee-keepers love the windbreak sycamore,
The twill of hanging flowers that the beech
Denies the yew – its waking life so long
It lets the stylish beechwood
Have its day, as winded oaks
Lay store upon their Lammas growth,
The thickening of their dreams.